Willia

A Midsummer Night's Dream

Retold by Helen Street
Illustrated by Charly Cheung

REAL
READS

Ernst Klett Sprachen
Stuttgart

First published in 2010 by Real Reads Ltd
Stroud, Gloucestershire, UK
www.realreads.co.uk

1. Auflage   1   5 4 3 2 1 | 2014 13 12 11 10

Alle Drucke dieser Auflage können nebeneinander benutzt werden, sie sind
untereinander unverändert. Die letzte Zahl bezeichnet das Jahr des Druckes.

Internetadresse: www.klett.de / www.lektueren.com

Umschlaggestaltung: Sandra Vrabec
Annotationen und Übungen: Rona McGeoch

Printed in China by Imago Ltd
Designed by Lucy Guenot
Typeset by Bookcraft Ltd, Stroud, Gloucestershire

ISBN 978-3-12-576195-7

9 783125 761957

CONTENTS

THE CHARACTERS

Hermia and Helena

Hermia and Helena are best friends so why would Helena betray her best friend's secret?

Lysander and Demetrius

Both are in love with Hermia, or are they? How will fairy magic affect their feelings for the two young women?

Egeus and the Duke of Athens

Egeus is Hermia's father, and can have her put to death if she refuses to marry Demetrius. Will the Duke overrule him so that Hermia can marry the man she loves?

Quince, Snug, Snout, Starveling and Flute

The workmen want to put on a play for the Duke, but they have problems – like what to do when the leading man disappears. Will their play ever be performed?

Nick Bottom

A weaver by trade, but an ass by nature. A fairy spell will make a donkey out of him.

The King and Queen of the Fairies

Oberon and Titania quarrel about a young boy she is caring for. Will Titania forgive her husband when he plays a trick on her?

Puck

Puck is the fairy king's cheeky servant who causes chaos amongst the lovers in the woods. Who will sort out the mess he has made?

5

A MIDSUMMER NIGHT'S DREAM

ACT ONE, SCENE ONE
HERMIA'S CHOICE

The Duke of Athens is in his palace when Egeus, a local businessman, enters, dragging along his daughter, Hermia. Two young men, Demetrius and Lysander, follow them.

Egeus

Noble duke, a humble servant greets you.

Duke

Welcome, Egeus. What brings you here to court?

Egeus

My daughter, lord, who will not me obey.

Come here, Demetrius. My noble lord,

This man has my consent to marry her.

Step forward, Lysander. My gracious duke,

Yet this one has bewitched my daughter's heart.

Duke

Hermia, what say you? Will you agree

To marry Demetrius? It is your father's wish.

The law is strict on disobedient maids.

Hermia

I must obey my heart – what is the law?

Duke

To die, or ever leave the world of men.

Hermia

Become a nun?

Duke

Aye, maid, that is the choice.

Hermia

Sooner a nun than that man's bride!

Duke

Come, come, sweet Hermia,

A lifetime singing hymns in a lonely cell

Compares not with the joys of married life.

Take time to think, and by the next new moon

Before this court pronounce your choice

To marry, die, or to become a nun.

Gentlemen, a word.

The Duke leaves with Egeus and Demetrius.

Hermia
It is the fate of lovers to be crossed,
Be thought too poor, too rich, too old, too young,
Or else not suited to a father's taste!

Lysander
The course of true love never did run smooth;
Yet even if all are happy with the choice,
War, death or sickness still may ruin all,
Making love momentary as a sound,
Swift as a shadow, short as any dream,
Brief as the lightning in the murky night.
I have a widowed aunt who lives outside
The city walls, some seven leagues at least,
Beyond the city and beyond its laws.
There, gentle Hermia, may I marry thee.
If you love me, creep from your father's house
Tomorrow night and meet me in the wood
Where once we met with Helena, your friend.
I will wait for you there.

Hermia
                    My good Lysander,
I swear to thee by Cupid's strongest bow
That to that place tomorrow I will go.

Helena walks past.

God speed, fair Helena! Don't go so soon.

Helena

Don't call me fair! Demetrius thinks not so.
He stole my heart yet gives his own to you.
I wish I had your looks, your smile, your voice,
So I might capture him the way you have.

Hermia

I frown upon him, yet he loves me still.
The more I hate, the more he follows me.

Helena

The more I love, the more he hateth me.

Hermia

Take comfort. He no more shall see my face.
Lysander and myself will leave this place.

Lysander

Helena, our secret we will share with you.
Tomorrow night, when moon shines full and bright
We meet in woods outside the city gates,
And then ...

Hermia

       Elope! And never will return.
Farewell, sweet playfellow. Pray thou for us,
And good luck grant thee thy Demetrius.

Hermia and Lysander leave.

Helena

I will tell Demetrius of their plan,
Then to the wood will he tomorrow night
Pursue her. And for this intelligence
If he gives thanks to me with some brief word
Then that will be reward enough for me.

Helena leaves.

ACT ONE, SCENE TWO
THE PLAYERS

Quince, Bottom, Snug, Flute, Snout and Starveling meet at Quince's cottage.

Quince

Masters, we shall perform a play to honour the noble Duke of Athens. I have the list of those who will take part. Is all our company here?

Bottom

First, good Peter Quince, say what the play is, then read the names of the actors.

Quince

Our play is 'The most lamentable comedy and most cruel death of Pyramus and Thisby'.

Bottom

An excellent play! Now, Peter Quince, call forth your actors. Masters, gather round.

Quince

Nick Bottom the weaver.

Bottom

Present!

Quince
You shall play Pyramus.

Bottom
What is Pyramus? A lover or a tyrant?

Quince
He is a lover who kills himself for love.

Bottom
O, I will have the audience in tears! I'll wail and weep and ... but I would rather play the tyrant and rant and rave about the stage like this:

'The raging rocks and shivering shocks
Shall break the locks of prison gates.
The blazing sun shall blind and stun
The hatless guard who stands and waits.'

Quince
Francis Flute, bellows-mender. You must take on Thisby.

Flute
What is Thisby? A wandering knight?

Quince
It is the lady Pyramus must love.

Flute

Not me! I have a beard coming on.

Quince

Fear not. You will wear a mask to hide your face.

Bottom

Let me play Thisby! I can speak in a woman's voice.
'Ah, Pyramus, my lover dear … '

Quince

No, no, you must play Pyramus. Robin Starveling,
the tailor?

Starveling

Here, Peter Quince.

Quince

You will play Thisby's mother, and Tom Snout the
tinker shall play Pyramus's father. Snug the joiner,
you will take the part of the lion.

Snug

Can I have my lines now? I am very slow at
learning.

Quince

All you have to do is roar.

Bottom

Let me play the lion! I can roar louder than any man.

Quince

Yes, and you would frighten the ladies and then the Duke would have us hung.

Snout

Yes, every one of us!

Bottom

O, but I will roar as gently as a dove – or a nightingale.

Quince

No, you must play Pyramus.

Bottom

Very well. Which beard shall I wear?

Quince

None, you shall play it barefaced, master Bottom. Now, masters. Here are your parts. Learn them and let us meet again tomorrow night in the palace wood. There we can rehearse in secret.

Bottom

Indeed. Let us meet and rehearse in our privates.

ACT TWO, SCENE ONE
THE FAIRY QUARREL

In the woods outside Athens. Puck enters.

Puck
The fairy king, my lord, comes here tonight.
'Tis hoped the fairy queen stays out of sight.
Their quarrelling has mixed the seasons up, and now
We know not if we'll have sun, or rain or snow.
And all for a pageboy who doth serve the queen,
For jealous Oberon would have the child
To live with him and roam the forest wild.

Oberon and Titania enter from different directions.

Oberon
Ill met by moonlight, proud Titania.

Titania
'Tis jealous Oberon. I will not stay!

Oberon

Give me the boy and I will go with thee.

Titania

Not for your fairy kingdom!

Oberon

                              Then go thy way.

Titania leaves.

But I shall pay thee for this stubbornness.
Puck, the flower, love-in-idleness, has
Magic juice that, touched on sleeping eyelids,
Will make a man or woman madly love
The first creature they set their eyes upon.
Fetch me that flower, and be thou here again
Before the giant whale can swim a league.

Puck

I'll put a girdle round about the earth
In forty minutes.

                              Puck leaves.

Oberon

                    When she is asleep,
I'll drop the juice in proud Titania's eye.
But who comes here? I am invisible,
And I will overhear their conversation.

                    Demetrius enters, followed by Helena.

Demetrius

I love thee not, therefore pursue me not!

Helena

I am your spaniel and, Demetrius,

The more you beat me I will fawn on you.

Use me but as your spaniel, spurn me, strike me,

Neglect me, lose me, only give me leave,

Unworthy as I am, to follow you.

Demetrius

I'll run from you and hide in the forest,

And leave you to the mercy of wild beasts.

Helena

No wild beast could be as cruel as you

Who tears my heart from me each time we meet.

Demetrius runs off, followed by Helena.

19

Oberon

Fear not, sweet maid, before he leaves this wood
He will come to love you as he should.

Puck reappears.

Did you bring the flower?

Puck

Yes, here it is.

Oberon

I know a bank whereon the wild thyme blows,
Where oxlips and the nodding violet grows,
Quite over-canopied with luscious woodbine,
With sweet musk-roses, and with eglantine:
There sleeps Titania sometime of the night,
Lulled in these flowers with dances and delight;
And with the juice of this I'll streak her eyes
And make her full of foolish fantasies.
Take some of this and search throughout the wood:
A disrespectful youth has spurned the love
Of some sweet maid who follows him.
Anoint his eyes to make him love her true,
And look thou meet me ere the first cock crow.

Puck

Fear not, my lord; your servant shall do so.

Puck and Oberon leave.

ACT TWO, SCENE TWO
PUCK'S MISTAKE

Titania lies asleep on the ground.
Oberon enters and anoints her eyes.

Oberon

When you wake, what first you see
Your very own true-love will be.

Oberon leaves. Hermia and Lysander enter.

Lysander

Fair love, you're tired from wandering in the wood,
And I confess I have forgot the way.
Let's rest here, Hermia, if you think it good,
And wait until dark night becomes bright day.

Hermia

So be it, Lysander. Go find a bed
For I upon this bank will lay my head.

They go to sleep some distance apart. Puck enters.

Puck

Through the forest I have gone
But Athenian found I none
On whose eyes I might approve
This flower's force in stirring love.

Night and silence – who is here?
Weeds of Athens he doth wear.
This is he, my master said,
Despised the Athenian maid.
And here the maiden, sleeping sound,
On the dank and dirty ground.
Pretty soul, she durst not lie
Near this lack-love, this kill-courtesy.
Churl, upon thy eyes I throw
All the power this charm doth owe.

Puck anoints Lysander's eyes, and leaves.
Helena enters.

Helena

O, I am out of breath in this fond chase,
And his long legs will help him win this race.
But who is here? Lysander! On the ground!
Dead? Or asleep? I see no blood, no wound.
Lysander, if you live, good sir, awake.

Lysander wakes up and sees Helena.

Lysander

And run through fire I will, for your sweet sake.
Vile Demetrius, who spurned you so;
I will cut out his heart to end your woe!

Helena

Speak not like that. His heart I do hold dear.
What matters it if he loves Hermia?
She loves you still, good friend, then be content.

Lysander

Content with Hermia? No: I do repent
The tedious minutes I with her have spent.
Not Hermia, but Helena I love –
Who will not change a raven for a dove?

Helena

Why do you play this cruel joke on me?
What harm I may have done you I can't see.
Then, I will say farewell. I must confess
I thought you lord of more true gentleness.

Helena leaves.

Lysander

O Hermia, sleep on there, do not wake.
With one last look my marriage pledge I break.
I hate you so. Let us keep far apart,
For only Helena shall have my heart.

Lysander follows Helena. Hermia wakes up.

Hermia

Help me, Lysander, help me; do thy best
To pluck this crawling serpent from my breast.
O! Just a dream, though now I am awake;
See thou, Lysander, how my pale hands shake.
Lysander? Where are you? Lysander! Say!
I see the place is empty where he lay.
Did a lion take him or is he lost?
I must now find my love whate'er the cost.

Hermia leaves.

ACT THREE, SCENE ONE
BOTTOM'S HEAD

In the wood, where Titania is asleep. Quince, Bottom, Snug, Starveling, Snout and Flute enter.

Quince

Here's a good spot for our rehearsal. Let's begin.

Bottom

A moment, master Quince. There are things in this play that will not do.

Quince

Tell, Bottom, what are they?

Bottom

First, Pyramus must draw a sword to kill himself. The ladies will faint at that.

Starveling

True, master Bottom. Then we must leave the killing out.

Bottom

No, I have a plan. Master Quince, you shall write a prologue.

Snug

What log is this?

Quince

A prologue – that is a speech before the play
begins.

Bottom

And it shall say that we will do no harm with
our swords and that I am not killed, and even
that I am not Pyramus who dies, but Bottom
the weaver.

Starveling

That will reassure the ladies indeed.

Snout

And will they not be afraid of the lion, too?

Bottom

Good point, master Snout.

Snug

Another log?

Bottom

No, you must show your face and speak directly
to the ladies and say, 'Do not fear, gentle ladies.
I am not a fierce lion, but only Snug the joiner.'

Flute

What shall we do for moonlight, for in the play Pyramus and Thisby meet by moonshine?

Bottom

Someone must enter with a candle and say he is the moon.

Quince

And what shall we do for a wall? The lovers must talk through a hole in a wall.

Snout

As big a problem as the lion!

Bottom

I have another plan for that. Someone must stand between them with his fingers outstretched like this, and they will speak as if they are the wall, and the space between their fingers the hole.

Quince

Then all is well. Now, masters, let us rehearse our parts. Bottom, you shall begin as Pyramus. And when you have said your speech, step behind that bush until it is your turn again.

Puck is hiding behind the bush.

Puck
What fools are these so near the Fairy Queen?
I'll do some mischief from a Puck unseen.

Bottom
'Thisby, the flowers smell of perfume sweat ...'

Quince
Perfume sweet ... !

Bottom
' ... of perfume sweet, so is the smell of your dear feet. But wait for me till I return. My heart for you will ever burn.'

Bottom goes behind the bush where Puck is watching.

Quince
Now, Flute, you must speak your lines as Thisby.

Flute
'O, Pyramus, where have you gone?'

Bottom comes back wearing a donkey's head.

Bottom

'I am here, sweet Thisby!'

Quince

Run, masters, run for your lives! It is a monster!

The workmen run away.

31

Bottom

I see their knavery. This is to make an ass out of me, to fright me if they could. But I will not stir from this place, do what they can. I will walk up and down here, and will sing that they shall hear I am not afraid.

> The ousel cock, so black of hue
> With orange-tawny bill,
> The throstle with his note so true,
> The wren with little quill.

Titania wakes up.

Titania

What angel wakes me from my flowery bed?

Bottom

> The finch, the sparrow, and the lark,
> The plain-song cuckoo grey,
> Whose note full many a man doth mark,
> And dares not answer nay.

Titania

A voice so sweet, and now my eyes
Look on a face so heavenly
That all at once I am in love
With this most strange and hairy god.

Bottom

I thank you, madam, though I am no more
handsome than the next fellow.

Titania

Not so, for you are beautiful to me,
And now I think my lover you shall be.
My fairies'll fetch you jewels from the deep
And sing, while you on perfumed flowers sleep.
They'll pluck the wings from painted butterflies
To fan the moonbeams from your sleeping eyes.

Titania leads Bottom away into the wood.

ACT THREE, SCENE TWO
THE LOVERS' QUARREL

Oberon and Puck meet in the same part of the wood.

Oberon

Here's my messenger. How now, mad spirit?

Puck

My mistress with a monster is in love!
While she was in her dull and sleeping hour,
A crew of patches, rude mechanicals,
Were met together to rehearse a play.
Upon one clumsy oaf I fixed a donkey's head
And in that moment (so it came to pass)
Titania waked and straightway loved an ass.

Oberon

O, this has turned out better than I hoped.
And have you yet bewitched the Athenian's eyes
With the love-juice as I did bid you do?

Puck

I found him sleeping – that is finished, too.
Demetrius and Hermia enter.

34

Oberon

Stand close; this is the same Athenian.

Puck

This is the woman, but not this the man.

Demetrius

Why are you cruel to one who loves you so,
And speak as if I were a bitter foe?

Hermia

If you have killed Lysander in his sleep,
Then take your sword and plunge it in my heart.
If he is dead, I do not wish to live.

Demetrius

I have not killed him, though if he were here
I'd take my sword and cut him ear to ear.

Hermia

Wicked Demetrius, now I will go.
See me no more, whether he be dead or no.

— *Hermia leaves.*

Demetrius

O, I am weary from this pointless chase.
I'll lay me down to sleep in this leafy place.

Demetrius goes to sleep.

Oberon

What mistake is this? Puck, what have you done?
Some other eyes, some other heart is won.
About the wood go swifter than the wind
And Helena of Athens look thou find.
By some illusion see thou bring her here,
I'll charm his eyes until she does appear.

> *Oberon anoints Demetrius's eyes. Puck returns,*
> *followed by Helena and Lysander.*

Puck

Helena, I bring to thee
And the youth mistook by me.

Oberon

Stand aside. The noise they make
Will cause Demetrius to awake.

Lysander

Why must you think I play a trick on you?
Are not these tears the proof my love is true?

Helena

It is not true, for yesterday your heart
Was pledged to Hermia, is that not so?

Lysander

If I loved her I was not in my mind!

Helena

You have lost it indeed to speak like this.

Lysander

Demetrius loves her, and he loves not you.

Demetrius wakes up and sees Helena.

Demetrius

O Helena, goddess, nymph, perfect, divine!
To what, my love, shall I compare thine eyne?
O princess fair, give me your hand to kiss;
Send me forever to a place of bliss!

Helena

O spite! O hell! I see you are all bent
To set against me for your merriment.
To vow, to swear, and superpraise my parts
When I am sure you hate me with your hearts.

Lysander

You are unkind, Demetrius, be not so –
For you love Hermia, this you know I know,
And I will give up Hermia's love to thee
If you will leave sweet Helena to me.

Demetrius

Lysander, keep thy Hermia, I will none.
If e'er I loved her, all that love is gone.

Hermia arrives, and rushes to Lysander.

Hermia

Thank the gods I've found you safe and well,
Your absence from me was a living hell.

Lysander

A hell it was if I had stayed with you!

Hermia

You do not know what you are saying, dear.

Helena

She is a willing part of their cruel game.
Ungrateful Hermia, have you forgot
The friendship we have known since we were young?
Like sisters have we been, loyal and true,
But now unkindness is your only gift.

Hermia

Helena, I am amazed at your words.
It is not I but you who are unkind.

Helena

Then why should these two men who love you, plead
False love for me but by your own command?

Hermia

I understand not what you mean by this.

Helena

Continue your pretence. Make faces now
At me behind my back. Yes, have your fun;
This maid has had enough. Farewell, false friends!

Lysander

Stay gentle Helena, do not go,
You are my life, my love, my heart, my soul!

Hermia

Lysander, do not tease her – it is cruel.

Demetrius

His love is false; all mine I pledge to you.

Lysander

Then draw your sword and we will see who's true.

Hermia

No, no, my love, I will not let you fight!

Lysander

Let go of me, you hag, and leave my sight.

Hermia

O Helena, what have you done, you thief?
You have stolen the heart that should be mine!

Helena

I have done nothing wrong, deserve no blame,
'Tis you, and they, who play this vicious game.

Hermia

Vicious? Why, I will show you vicious, maid!

Hermia runs at Helena.

Helena

Gentlemen, save me, though you mock me still.

When she is angry, she is keen and shrewd.

She was a vixen when she went to school,

And though she be but little she is fierce.

Hermia

Take that back or I will come at thee!

Lysander *(to Hermia)*

Get you gone, you pipsqueak, you vile thing!

Demetrius

Nay, I shall be the one to take her part.

Lysander

Think you so? Then let us fight a duel
Elsewhere, and you may prove yourself to me!

Demetrius

Agreed! The winner shall have Helena's hand.

*Demetrius and Lysander leave together
with swords drawn.*

Hermia

You, mistress! This is all because of you!

Helena

I will not stay to let you scratch my face,
But run away from this unhappy place.

Helena runs off.

Hermia

I am amazed and know not what to say.

Hermia walks off.

Oberon

This is your doing, O mischievous sprite!
Something must be done to put things right.
Bring down a mist about this wood so thick
That none shall see their hand before their face.

Puck

With false calls I will lead each man astray,
So none be harmed on this midsummer's night.

Oberon

When they at last do fall asleep, this herb
Into Lysander's eye do crush it well.
Its juice will right the wrong that has been done,
And when the lovers wake and meet at dawn
It shall be as if they had but dreamt a dream.
Go, work your magic on these mortals, Puck.
I'll to the Fairy Queen, demand the boy,
And lift the love charm from her eyes. Haste!

Puck and Oberon leave.

ACT FOUR
BOTTOM IS RESTORED

Outside the palace. The workmen enter.

Quince

Have you been to Bottom's house? Is he come home yet?

Starveling

He cannot be heard of.

Snug

He has been carried off for sure, masters, and we will never see him again!

Flute

But how are we to perform our play?

Quince

It cannot be done without Bottom.

Bottom enters, looking normal again.

Bottom

What cannot be done? For I, Bottom, am here!

The workmen greet him with surprise and joy.

I've had a wondrous adventure, but I shall tell
you no more for now. But put on your costumes,
tie on your beards and lace up your shoes, for
there is a play to be done. Hurry, masters, the
lords and ladies are waiting!

*The workmen exit as the Duke and Egeus enter from
one side and the lovers arrive from the other.*

Duke

Good day, young friends.
You all seem touched with joy.

Lysander

My lord, we all have had the strangest dream
In which we loved first one fair maid, and then
The other seemed still fairer yet to us.
Now all is resolved. Demetrius
And Helena have found true love at last.
And Hermia and I have pledged our hearts.
And so, my lord, we ask consent to wed.

Egeus

I beg the law! The law upon his head!
Demetrius shall have my daughter's hand.

Demetrius

I only wish for Helena's sweet love.
If she will have me, Duke, I ask your leave
For us to marry, too.

Helena

                  O, yes, my love!

Duke

Egeus, I will override your will.
These happy couples shall this day be wed
At my command. Come to the palace, all,
To feast and celebrate the power of love.

             All exit together.

ACT FIVE
THE WORKMEN'S PLAY

The palace. The Duke, Egeus, Lysander, Hermia,
Demetrius and Helena are all sitting and waiting.

Duke

What entertainment have we for tonight?

Egeus

Some workmen, lord, who would perform
a play.

Duke

Then bid them begin.

Egeus

                I have seen them act.
A worse performance there has never been!

Duke

Then we shall have some fun at their expense.
Snout enters as Wall, and holds up his hands
in a mime of a wall.

Snout

I am Wall and through this gap, the lovers
Thisby and Pyramus must whisper their love.

Bottom enters as Pyramus.

Bottom

Good sirs and ladies, too. I am Pyramus and
now I will speak.

O darkest night! O night so black!

O night, o night! Alack! Alack!

Duke

'Tis safe to say it is night!

Bottom

Thisby, my love, where are you?

Flute enters as Thisby.

Flute

Here, my love, behind this wall that ever keeps
our hearts apart!

Bottom

O kiss me through the hole of this vile wall.

Flute tries to kiss through the gap in Snout's fingers.

Flute

I kiss the wall's hole, not your lips at all.

Hermia

A more handsome man than Pyramus, I think!

Bottom

Meet me then at Ninny's tomb.

Flute

I go, I fly, I'll be there soon!

Bottom and Flute exit in opposite directions.

Snout

My part now is finished and so Wall bids you farewell.

Snout exits. Snug enters as Lion,
and Starveling as Moonshine.

Snug

Ladies, be not afraid. I am not a real lion but Snug the joiner. I am a gentle soul and mean you no harm.

Starveling

Lords – and ladies – the lovers must have moonlight to meet by. Therefore, this here lantern shall be the moon and I am the man in the moon.

Lysander

Then there is some mistake, for he should be inside the lantern.

Demetrius

He is afraid of being burned!

Flute enters.

Flute

Where is my love?

Lion roars and grabs Thisby's cloak.
'She' runs away screaming. Lion runs off.

Lysander

Well roared, Lion.

Helena

Well run, Thisby.

Hermia

Well shone, Moon.

Demetrius

And then came Pyramus ...

Bottom enters.

Bottom

Sweet moon, I thank thee for thy sunny beams!
That light me to the woman of my dreams.
But wait! What is this? My Thisby's cloak all
stained with blood? A vile beast has killed my love!
O woe is me! Alack! Alack!

Duke

There is certainly a lack of something here!

Bottom

Come, sword, and stab the heart of Pyramus! I die.

Egeus

I wish he would.

Bottom

Now am I dead, now am I fled;

My soul is in the sky.

Tongue, lose they light! Moon, take thy flight!

Now die, die, die, die – die!

Duke

Thanks be for that.

Flute enters.

Flute

Asleep, my love? What, dead, my dove?

Come, sword, and do your worst.

Thisby 'dies' over the body of Pyramus.
Lion and Moonshine drag off the bodies.

Duke

Moonshine and Lion are left to bury the dead.

Egeus

They should have buried the play!

Duke

The iron tongue of midnight hath told twelve!

Lovers to bed – 'tis almost fairy time.

They all leave. Oberon, Titania and Puck enter.

Puck

Now the hungry lion roars,

And the wolf behowls the moon;

Whilst the heavy ploughman snores,

All with weary task fordone.

Oberon

Now, until the break of day,
Through this house each fairy stray.

Titania

Hand in hand, with fairy grace,
Will we sing and bless this place.

Puck

If we shadows have offended,
Think but this, and all is mended,
That you have but slumbered here
While these visions did appear,
And this weak and idle theme
No more yielding but a dream.

Taking things further

Glossary

Abbreviations:
opp of *opposite of*
old *old-fashioned*
usu *usually*
e.g. *for example*
sb *somebody*
sth *something*

Page 4

to betray *verraten*
fairy (*usu* good) human-like being with magical powers
duke *Herzog*
to refuse *opp of* to agree (to)
to overrule *überstimmen*

Page 5

leading man *Hauptdarsteller*
weaver by trade *Weber von Beruf*
ass donkey, *here (old):* a silly person
by nature *von Natur aus*
spell magical words
to quarrel ['kwɒrəl] to argue, to fight
cheeky *frech*
to cause sth to make sth happen
amongst *unter*
the woods forest

Page 7

to drag to pull behind you
humble *bescheiden, demütig*
court *Gericht*
to obey sb to do what sb wants you to do
consent agreement
gracious *gütig, gnädig*
bewitched [bɪ'wɪtʃt] changed by magic *(verzaubert)*
disobedient not behaving as told to
maid *(old)* unmarried woman

Page 8

ever *here:* forever
sooner a nun I'd rather be a nun *(Nonne)*
bride woman on her wedding day
cell small, basic room (*usu* in a prison)
to pronounce *verkünden*

Page 9

fate *Schicksal*
to be crossed *(old)* to have bad luck
to suit to be right for *(passen)*
course the path, the way sth goes
momentary only lasting for a moment
swift fast, quick
brief short
murky dark, unclear
widowed whose husband has died
league [liːg] *(old)* unit of distance (about 5 km)
beyond past, on the other side of
to creep to move quietly, not wanting to be seen or heard
to swear to promise
Cupid Roman god of love *(Amor)*

Page 10

God speed *(old) Gott sei mit dir*
looks sb's appearance
to capture to catch and hold
frown upon *here:* to dislike

Page 11

bright *opp of* dark *(hell)*
to elope to run away to get married
playfellow *(old)* friend to play with
to pray to talk to God *(beten)*
to grant to give
to pursue [pə'sjuː] to follow
intelligence *here:* secret information
reward *Belohnung*

Page 12

cottage a small, simple house
to honour ['ɒnə] *ehren*
company *here:* group of actors
lamentable ['læməntəbl] *beklagenswert*
cruel *grausam*
to call forth *(old)* to read out
to gather round to come together
present *anwesend*

to wail to make a loud, unhappy noise

to weep to cry

to rant and rave to shout angrily

to rage to shout loudly and angrily

to shiver to shake because of cold or fear

lock sth to keep sth closed *(Schloss)*

blazing burning/shining brightly

to stun to shock so that sb/sth cannot move or speak

guard sb who watches and protects sth

bellows-mender *(old)* sb who repairs broken bellows *(Blasebalg)*

to take on *here:* to play

to wander to walk around without an aim

tailor sb whose job it is to make clothes *(Schneider)*

tinker *(old)* sb who mends broken things *(Kesselflicker)*

joiner sb whose job it is to make things from wood *(Schreiner)*

lines text of a character in a play

to roar (of an animal) to make a loud noise

to hang (hung, hung) to kill sb by hanging him/her from a rope

dove [dʌv] *Taube*

nightingale ['naɪtɪŋɡeɪl] *Nachtigall*

barefaced without a beard

to rehearse [rɪ'hɜːs] to practise

indeed *allerdings*

in our privates *(old)* on our own

pageboy servant boy at a royal court

jealous wanting sth that sb else has *(eifersüchtig)*

would have *(old)* would like to have

to roam to walk around without an aim

proud *stolz, hochmütig*

kingdom area ruled by a king

stubbornness *Sturheit*

love-in-idleness *(old) Wildes Stiefmütterchen*

juice *here:* liquid inside a plant's stem or leaves

to set your eyes upon to look at

to fetch to bring sth to sb

girdle *(old)* belt

invisible not possible to be seen *(unsichtbar)*

to overhear to listen to secretly

to beat to hit hard

to fawn on sb *(old)* to show a lot of love for

to spurn *(old)* to reject, to turn away

to strike to hit hard

to neglect to not pay sb enough attention

to give sb leave to allow

mercy *Gnade, Barmherzigkeit*

beast large wild animal

to tear to pull at sth roughly

bank side of a river or hill

thyme *Thymian*

to blow *here:* to move in the wind

oxlip *Hohe Schlüsselblume*

nodding moving the head (*here:* the heads of the flowers)

violet *Veilchen*

over-canopied covered as if by a roof

luscious ['lʌʃəs] very sweet-smelling

woodbine type of climbing plant

eglantine *Heckenrose*

lulled calmed

delight joy, happiness

to streak *here:* to touch

throughout all through

to anoint to touch sb with e.g. oil *(einsalben)*

cock *Hahn*

to crow *krähen*

to confess to admit
forgot (to forget) forgotten
upon on top of
Athenian sb from Athens
to approve to find good
force power
to stir *here:* to awaken, to create

weeds *here:* clothes
to despise to dislike strongly, to hate
sound *here:* deeply
dank wet and cold
durst not *(old)* is not brave enough to
lack-love *(old)* heartless person
kill-courtesy ['kɜːtəsi] *(old)* rude person
churl *(old)* unpleasant, unkind man
charm magic spell, sth with magical powers
doth owe *(old)* owns, has got

out of breath *außer Atem*
fond *(old) here:* silly
chase running after sb/sth *(Jagd)*
wound [wuːnd] injury *(Verletzung)*
for sb's sake for sb, to please sb
vile horrible, evil
woe unhappiness
to repent to regret *(bereuen)*
tedious ['tiːdiəs] boring
raven type of bird *(Rabe)*

harm damage *(Schaden)*
I thought you lord of I thought you had
marriage pledge *(old)* promise to marry
to keep apart to stay away from each other
to pluck *(old)* to pick, to pull
crawling moving on the stomach or hand and knees
serpent *(old)* snake
breast [brest] *Brust*
pale light in colour

to draw to pull out
sword [sɔːd] long, sharp weapon *(Schwert)*
to faint to become unconscious
prologue ['prəʊlɒg] *Prolog*

log *Baumstamm*
to reassure to calm, to make (sb) feel better
fierce aggressive

outstretched stretched out *(ausgestreckt)*

fool stupid person
mischief ['mɪstʃɪf] *(old) Unfug*
unseen not seen
sweat [swet] *Schweiß*

knavery ['neɪvəri] *(old)* tricks
to fright *(old)* to frighten
to stir to move
ousel ['uːzəl] *(old)* blackbird *(Amsel)*
hue *(old)* colour
orange-tawnery *(old)* orange-brown
bill mouth of a bird *(Schnabel)*
throstle note so true clear song of the thrush *(Drossel)*
wren [ren] *Zaunkönig*
little quill *(old)* quiet song
finch *Fink*
sparrow *Spatz*
lark *Lerche*
note musical sound *(Ton)*
doth mark notices
to dare to be brave enough to

heavenly *himmlisch*
hairy covered in hair
handsome ['hændsəm] good-looking (of a man)
fellow *(old)* man
perfumed sweet smelling
to fan *fächern*
moonbeam *Mondstrahl*

57

Page 34

messenger sb who delivers a message

How now? *(old) Was soll das bedeuten?*

spirit *Geist*

crew of patches *(old)* group of clowns

rude mechanicals simple workmen

were met did meet

clumsy oaf careless, stupid person

came to pass *(old)* happened

straightway at once

to bid *(old)* to ask

Page 35

foe *(old)* enemy

to plunge to push sth in very hard

wicked cruel, bad

weary *(old)* tired

pointless making no sense

leafy full of leaves

Page 36

swifter faster

to see *here:* to make sure

mistook *verwechselt*

proof sth that shows sth to be true

to pledge to promise

Page 37

nymph *Nymphe*

divine god-like *(göttlich)*

thine eyne *(old)* your eyes

bliss happiness

Page 38

spite *Bosheit, Gehässigkeit*

to be bent *auf etwas erpicht sein*

to set against sb to be against sb

for your merriment *(old)* to entertain yourselves

to vow to promise

to superpraise to praise too much

absence not being present *(Abwesenheit)*

Page 39

willing *bereit, gewillt*

ungrateful not showing thanks

unkindness not being friendly

to be amazed to be very surprised

plead claim

command order *(Befehl)*

pretence pretending *(Vortäuschung)*

Page 40

to tease to annoy

hag old, unattractive woman

vicious [ˈvɪʃəs] nasty

Page 41

to mock to make fun of *(hänseln)*

keen clever

shrewd [ʃruːd] *scharfsinnig*

vixen woman who likes to argue

get you gone go away

pipsqueak unimportant person

Page 42

to prove yourself *sich bewähren*

to scratch to tear the skin

Page 43

your doing your fault

mischievous *schelmisch*

sprite fairy

to lead sb astray to make sb lose his/her way

to crush *ausdrücken, auspressen*

to right to make sth OK again

mortal *Sterblicher*

Page 46

wonderous amazing

to lace up to tie (of shoe laces)

touched *ergriffen, gerührt*

to have sb's hand to be allowed to marry sb

Page 47

leave permission

to override to decide against

at my command because I say so

to feast to have a good meal

at sb's expense *auf jmds. Kosten*
mime acting without speaking
gap hole

apart away from each other

tomb [tuːm] place where a dead
body is put *(Grab)*
to bid sb farewell to say goodbye
to sb
this here *(old)* this
lantern light which can be carried

to grab to take sth quickly
cloak old-fashioned type of coat
(Umhang)
beam *Lichtstrahl*
to light to light up
stained made dirty
woe is me poor me
certainly surely

to bury to put a dead person
under the ground *(beerdigen)*
iron tongue [aɪən tʌŋ] *eiserne
Zunge, here:* hand of a clock
to behowl to howl to *(anheulen)*
ploughman [ˈplaʊmən] *Pflüger*
to snore to breathe noisily while
sleeping
fordone *(old)* very tired

to stray to walk around
(somewhere where you don't belong)
to bless *segnen*
to offend to make angry *(beleidigen)*
but *(old)* just, only
to slumber to sleep deeply
no more yielding but nothing more
than

Exercises

Act one

Comprehension

Answer these questions from the text.

1. Describe the opening situation.

2. What choices does the Duke offer Hermia and why?

3. How does Hermia react?

4. What does Lysander suggest?

5. What is Helena's problem?

6. What does Helena plan to do and why?

7. Why are the players meeting?

Characters

Who loves whom? Who doesn't love whom? Fill in the diagram.

Hermia   Helena   Lysander   Demetrius

Hermia   Lysander

Helena   Demetrius

Language

Choose suitable adjectives from the box to finish the sentences.

disobedient   smooth   secret   strict   hopeful   annoyed

1. Egeus is very .... with his daughter.
2. He thinks she's being ....
3. The Duke says that the law is very ....
4. Lysander complains that the course of true love never did run

   ....
5. Lysander and Hermia agree on a .... plan.
6. Helena is .... that if she tells Demetrius, he might like her.

60

Comprehension

Answer these questions from the text.

1. Who are Oberon and Titania and what is the situation between them?

2. What is so special about love-in-idleness?

3. Which two things does Oberon plan to do?

4. Describe Puck's mistake.

5. How does Helena react to Lysander's behaviour?

6. What happens when Hermia wakes up?

Language

Finish the sentences.

1. If Oberon and Titania hadn't been quarrelling, ...
....

2. If Demetrius had not run away, ...
....

3. If Lysander and Hermia hadn't fallen asleep, ...
....

4. If Puck hadn't made a mistake, ...
....

5. If Helena hadn't arrived, ...
....

6. If Hermia had woken up first, ...
....

Act out

Work in groups of three. Imagine Hermia wakes up in the middle of the conversation between Lysander and Helena. How does she react? How does Helena react? Write a script for the conversation and then act it out.

Act three

Language

Find words to match these definitions.

1. a speech before the play begins ....

2. to make somebody feel safe (again) ....

3. aggressive ....

4. good-looking (of a man) ....

5. ugly, old woman ....

6. very surprised ....

Diary Entry

Write Helena's diary entry. How does she describe what happens? How does she feel about the other characters? Start like this:

I can't believe what happened today - . . .

Characters

What has changed? Who loves whom now? Who doesn't love whom now? Fill in the diagram.

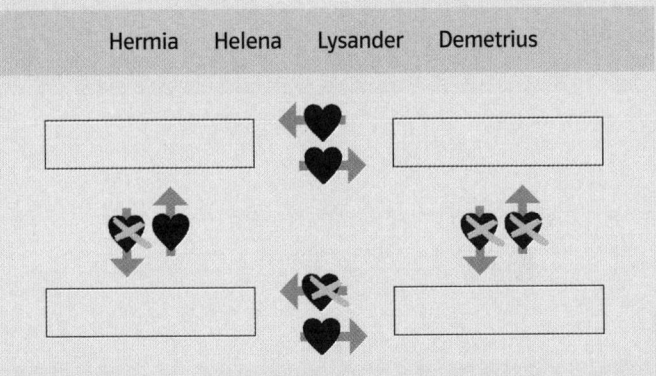

| Hermia | Helena | Lysander | Demetrius |

Act four

Comprehension

Answer these questions from the text.

1. What is the problem at the beginning of Act four?

2. What does Bottom say has happened to him?

3. What do the couples think has happened?

4. What does Egeus want?

5. What does the Duke decide?

Act out

Work in pairs. Write a script for a dialogue between Egeus and Demetrius, in which Egeus asks Demetrius why he has suddenly changed his mind. Act out the scene.

Comprehension

Answer these questions from the text.

1. What does Egeus say about the actors?

2. What does Lysander say is wrong, and how does Demetrius explain this?

3. What happens after twelve?

4. What does Puck say at the end?

Language

Translate these passages into modern English.

1. 'Tis safe to say it is night! ....

2. O woe is me! Alack! Alack! ....

3. The iron tongue of midnight hath told twelve! ....
   ....

Characters – Who belongs to whom?

Make a list of characters in the play. Now sort them into three groups. Which characters are Athenians? Which are fairy people? Which are workmen / actors?

Athenians	fairy people	workmen / actors